Chuckles

JAN TRABUE

Licensed Professional Clinical Counselor

ISBN 978-1-66785-676-6 (Print)

ISBN 978-1-66785-677-3 (eBook)

Here's the Story...

A wild white squirrel I named MartyLou is the sole character in each *smile maker* included in this book. I have been photographing MartyLou for several years now and have used my images to create children's therapeutic books. I began creating these *smile makers* 2 years ago and have accumulated quite a few over the years. These have made me smile often! My motivation for creating this book is to cause you to smile and of course, chuckle! Use of humor is an important coping strategy to help us deal with unsettling situations, people, events, or random social factors. When we can laugh at the irony often present in day to day life, we can then shift the perspective we have from one that may be grounded in frustration, impatience, anger, or any other unpleasant emotion, to one that allows us to see and maybe gain some understanding of the other side.

Additionally, use of humor through these *smile makers* often validate something we personally think or have feelings about. When we view something that makes us smile and we declare, "Yes! That's me! That's how I feel too!" we feel validated and understood. Feeling validated and understood goes a long way to helping us feel more empowered to deal with a situation or change it!

easy
breezy
beautiful

Cover
Squirrel

3

Car 10 feet from me

4

I should totally cross the road now

BELL RANG

GOT WINGS

♪♫ **It's a squirrel my lord in a flatbed Ford, slowing down to take a look at me** ♫♪

6

Excuse me, Jan,
could I please have a generous portion
of assorted, premium nuts?
I'll need that to go please.

7

YEAH, I'M INTO FITNESS

FITNESS WHOLE NUT IN MY MOUTH

Run! Friday the 13th is coming!

9

Fist bump, bro

Me eating as much as I want before I commit to a New Year's resolution to lose weight

11

Thought about going to yoga

but then I thought, namaste here and do some postures

12

What happens when you don't pre-plan your meals

13

When you already started to eat

14

and someone says, "Let's pray."

MARCHING INTO THE NEW YEAR LIKE A BOSS!

15

I was told

16

there would be privilege?

I will hold him and squeeze him
and hug him and pet him
and call him Tree.

17

I hate that time
in the morning
when I have to get up

So it's Monday

just roll with it

19

JOY
TO
THE
SQUIRREL

20

Just a cup or two of coffee to help me deal with a bunch of nuts today

Hello,

is it me you're looking for?

23

Not all superheroes wear a cape

A SQUIRREL WHEN A PERSON LOOKS AT THEM

A SQUIRREL WHEN A CAR GOING 60 MPH IS ABOUT TO HIT THEM

WHen I learned,
'You are what
you eat,'

26

I realized I WAS NUTS!

I may seem okay

but deep down inside I can't remember all of my passwords

27

Just stop talking

28

I'm sure whatever you want to say can wait til you're smarter

WHEN SOMEONE GIVES ME DIRECTIONS AND USES WORDS LIKE EAST

What do you mean I can't wear white after Labor Day?

When you catch yourself just as you're about to experience a fate worse than death

Me after a day of peopling

Gee my hair smells terrific!

WHEN I TRY TO LOG ONTO AN APP AND I GET THE MESSAGE, "YOUR PASSWORD OR USERNAME IS INCORRECT."

WELL, WHICH ONE IS IT?!

WITCHING YOU A FA-BOO-LOUS HALLOWEEN

When you care more
about food than people

so you pretend
to be interested
in what they're saying

36

They sit at the bar and put nuts in
my jar and say,
"Squirrel, what are you doing here?"

37

When someone asks me which is more important food or people-

I dont answer because Im too busy eating

38

Girls dig me

because of my resounding sax appeal

39

Don't give up on your dreams

Keep on sleeping

40

That awkward silence when someone asks you a question just when you shoved food in your mouth

41

and they wait for you to stop chewing

Always use your turn signal to avoid having a wreck